T0158169

River of Time

Six Seasons of Tanka

Robert W. Barker

iUniverse, Inc.
Bloomington

River of Time

Six Seasons of Tanka

iUniverse books may be ordered through booksellers or by contacting:

iUniverse
1663 Liberty Drive
Bloomington, IN 47403
www.iuniverse.com
1-800-Authors (1-800-288-4677)

ISBN: 978-1-4759-3754-1 (sc)
ISBN: 978-1-4759-3755-8 (ebk)

Printed in the United States of America

iUniverse rev. date: 07/17/2012

To Cynthia,

For her love and courage.

To Hope,

For her gift of the future.

Their spirit remains,

In the corners of the room,

Memories held, tight.

But they forge their own lives now;

Old bonds forever broken.

January 3, 2011
Visit of a grown child

Drop pebbles softly,

Into life's dark, limpid pool.

Ripples form, vanish,

Waking our souls in passage;

Reaching, drop one, round pebble.

January 28, 2011
Consequences

Relaxing my grasp,

I let the small bird fly free;

And I watch, afraid.

Frantic wings carry her home;

Without wings, I am still, lost.

March 10, 2011
Going home

Dawn breaks with night snow,

Breathless and weightless, clinging

To silent branches.

Under overhung tree limbs,

We hold our breath, for the wind.

March 18, 2011
Late winter snow

Surprised by each dawn,

Every joy unpredicted,

Sorrows lost in sand;

In the winter of our lives,

Savor all, undiluted.

March 23, 2011
Live fully

Burn the holy book;

In Christ's own name, burn the book,

In the name of love.

Where is this God, so hate filled?

Who kills, for windblown ashes?

April 2, 2011
Another Jones

SPRING

Shackled to the rocks;

Crashing waves or rising tide,

Drowning is the same.

Let the spirit currents flow,

And float free upon the sea.

April 10, 2011
Break free

Memories, cherish;

They are no longer living.

Let them go, gently.

Turn, dismiss the gentle life;

Enter the race, strong once more.

April 11, 2011
Loss becomes beginning

What grips my heart now?

No fond emotion, no joy,

Just old, lonesome fear.

I am consumed by living,

With a lust to live life well.

April 13, 2011
Chest pains

Tangled in my web,

Built step by step, with such care;

It traps me, holds me.

Forbidding, dangerous ground;

Abandon all, and step free.

April 19, 2011
New vision

All consuming noise,

Quiet now, the floors echo.

The soul departed.

The rustling husk still remains,

But our lives move quickly on.

April 28, 2011
Closing the house

The views are changing,

New and unfamiliar scenes,

Confront us daily.

The folds of our lives ripple,

Shaking the old foundations.

April 30, 2011
Transitions

Young leaves, blinding green,

Too clear, sharp, for human eyes,

They speak of ages.

One glimpse, and now, forever,

Lost, in creation's maelstrom.

May 8, 2011
Rebirth

With its empty eyes,

The bare elk skull stares at me,

Challenging my life.

Picked clean in death, long ago,

I refuse the dry rebuke.

May 23, 2011
Death and life

Image on image,

Those we love and hardly know;

We are surrounded.

Waiting for our lives to turn,

Our embraces come too late.

May 27, 2011
Regrets

Staring from the screen,

Quiet, direct, unmoving;

Who is this stranger?

Distant, across space and time,

I reach out, and greet myself.

May 29, 2011
Photographs

SUMMER

The old house is gone;

Only children's dreams remain,

To live, forgotten.

Hedges, planted years ago,

Still bloom in white profusion.

June 1, 2011
Forgotten dreams

Fight for justice now?

Our violent wars prevent us;

Revenge, bathed in blood.

Captured by bright illusion,

We destroy our tortured world.

June 7, 2011
Pox Americana

Waves crash endlessly;

Palms stand green against blue sky;

Quiet paradise.

The violence of our habits,

Softly whispers in the breeze.

June 9, 2011
Mexico denial

Images flicker,

Starving children wait to die,

Hopeless, so alone.

Death will embrace the children,

Like their parents, gone before.

June 13, 2011
Ghetto images

I believe in life,

In the next generation,

In youth blossoming.

I must believe that they can

Save the world, from all my sins.

June 14, 2011
Hope

Stand naked, shiver,

Bright stars pierce the velvet dark;

There are spirits here.

A dog barks; he senses them.

Ancient, they caress my soul.

June 17, 2011
Peru memories

Mountain views, unseen,

Hidden in the fog and mist;

Groping for landmarks.

I know this place, from long past;

Blind, I seek my home again.

June 29, 2011
Seeking

Together we fly,

Racing across the green land,

A distant vision.

Together for the first time,

We become one, unified.

July 6, 2011
The joining

Set the new patterns;

Slowly, all the pieces join,

Opening pathways.

Surrounded by our history,

We begin, the beginning.

July 13, 2011
Making it home

The full moon rises,

Guided by the twin trunked oak;

Pausing, suspended.

Dark leaves, sharp against the light,

Beautiful, so swiftly passed.

July 15, 2011
Full moon

Frog voices calling,

Breaking the soft, dark silence;

Echoes in moonlight.

Listen to the ancient call,

Still waiting, hopeful, for life.

July 17, 2011
Frogs at night

Gray, flat light descends

Upon the living city,

Covering all sins.

My soul, no longer bleeding,

Welcomes the growing softness.

July 28, 2011
Toronto fog

Quick flash, black on red,

Color turns again to song;

Blazing, tiny heart.

The small, bright bird fills my soul,

Lost so many years ago.

August 3, 2011
Scarlet tanager

Lost in emptiness,

Western sky glows burnt orange,

Black palm silhouettes.

Life flows by in noise and dust,

Leaving us invisible.

August 7, 2011
Paraguay at night

The long steady rain,

Creates gray, ghostly meadows,

In fading twilight.

Old fields, now grown high with weeds,

Sigh with farmers' memories.

August 17, 2011
Dead farm

A small broken man,

Reaches, pulls music gently,

From the old violin.

Just a simple box with strings,

Until his heart sets it free.

August 28, 2011
Pearlman, Tanglewood

The stream is larger.

Though still quiet, well behaved,

It has more—presence.

I will never own this stream;

Surely it possesses me.

August 30, 2011
Sound of water

Dark and quiet night,

Uncounted stars pierce the black,

Each a miracle.

We have seen bright galaxies;

And reaching, touched creation.

September 5, 2011
Creation's reach

FALL

Living harvest time,

Young lives, with such abundance;

Racing fearlessly.

Time may bring its empty fields,

But time holds no fear for youth.

September 12, 2011
Young life

Cool, sweet kiss of fall,

Clears the air of summer haze;

Small groves of color,

Give thoughts of frozen darkness,

Long and empty, winter's night.

September 17, 2011
Endings

Patiently she sits,

And holds their worlds together,

As he loses his;

Leaving, she turns, touches me,

"Pray you do not die this way."

September 18, 2011
Alzheimers

Delicate circles,

Lightly traced across the sky,

Effortless beauty;

Stopping to rest in the oak,

She tilts her bald head, and stares.

September 20, 2011
Vulture

After rainfall ends,

Rainbows dance against the clouds,

Shifting with the sun.

Newly washed, wind rattles leaves,

Carrying scents of green grass.

September 29, 2011
Autumn rain

EARLY WINTER

Fog fills the valley,

As the white seas of my dreams;

I accept comfort.

Softly rocking on the waves,

Yesterday's forgetfulness.

November 9, 2011
The day after

You are gone, missing;

I yell, softly, this is hell!

But I know I'm wrong.

I've visited there, before,

When I told you of my sins.

November 19, 2011
Separation

Familiar faces,

Furrowed with swift, passing time,

Longing for old love.

We tell our stories, and still,

We dream. Futures, yet to be.

November 27, 2011
Family gathering

Long ago, so young,

I once felt your secret thoughts,

Touching my hot soul.

Today, ancient memories,

Still sharp, still pain, still treasure.

November 28, 2011
Memories of youth

In the dark valley,

Frost clings to dry, brittle grass,

In late morning shade.

Drifting smoke, from early fires,

Carries soft, family whispers.

December 4, 2011
Living darkly

There, lonely snowflakes,

Falling slowly, softly down,

Is it white Christmas?

The snow, so faint, like my thoughts,

For this day of miracles.

December 25, 2011
Christmas morning

THE SECOND
LATE WINTER

Tiny, hidden child,

Growing swiftly, limb by limb,

Life's true miracle.

The future forms quietly,

Soon to take its rightful place.

January 3, 2012
Life's miracle

An old friend, drowning,

Unable to save himself,

Slowly drifts away.

Calling, he does not hear me;

Reaching, I do not find him.

January 27, 2012
Life's losses

The stories haunt me,

Leaping out from bright, white walls,

Torture, fierce anger.

We have sown our bitter seeds;

Now we harvest full grown hate.

January 30, 2012
Guantanamo

Another presence

Lies between us in our bed.

I tremble, afraid.

Touch her, hold her, tenderly;

Walk life's pathways, together.

February 5, 2012
Love's testing

The last leaves are gone.

The oak stands truly naked,

Stripped by passing wind.

Against cold winds, we two stand,

Still entangled by our love.

February 13, 2012
Stripped to essence

I watch, quietly,

Outside, not allowed entry,

Alone with my fears.

All I have for her is love,

And two strong arms to hold her.

February 17, 2012
Testing day

Speaking with silence,

Soft fatigue has settled here.

Quietly, we wait,

Leaving our thoughts unuttered.

Holding, touching, one more time.

February 26, 2012
Love's touch

THE
CURRENTS
STILL FLOW